INFORMANIA

ALIENS

.on

About This Book

Addicted to aliens? You're about to be! Here's everything you've ever wanted to know about extraterrestrials — and some things you've never even dreamed of!

Section 1 . . . page 5
Fantastic UFO Sightings

Have an uncommonly close encounter in this sensational exposé of UFO sightings. What do witnesses claim aliens look like? Are there any real-life Men in Black? You'll find all the answers and more in my special edition of BEYOND BELIEF magazine!

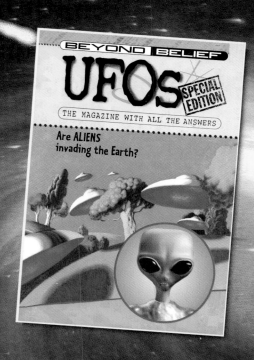

BEYOND BELIEF

UFOS SPECIAL EDITION

THE MAGAZINE WITH ALL THE ANSWERS

Are ALIENS invading the Earth?

SPACE CADET SCHOOL

ENTRANCE EXAMINATION

LOOK TO THE FUTURE —
BE A PART OF THE SEARCH FOR ALIEN LIFE!

Section 2 . . . page 29
Is Alien Life Possible?

To get to the bottom of this mind-boggling mystery, I set up the Space Cadet School. Then I borrowed its star student's entrance examination paper — to find out whether life really might exist anywhere else in the Universe besides Earth.

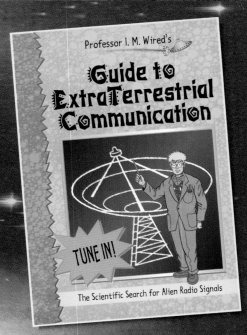

Professor I. M. Wired's

Guide to ExtraTerrestrial Communication

TUNE IN!

The Scientific Search for Alien Radio Signals

Section 3... page 51
Tips on Talking to Aliens

Wish you could call up E.T.? Tune in to the wired-up world of radio astronomy and come to grips with SETI, the Search for ExtraTerrestrial Intelligence. Discover how we're listening for alien messages — and what we'd do if we found one!

Section 4... page 71
Aliens in the Movies

I asked movie buff Michael Johnstone to put on his casting agent's hat and give us the lowdown on his all-time favorite film-star aliens — some are weird, some are wacky, and some are downright dangerous!

MIKEY
Hiram called — can you put the casting notes in the post today!

MIKEY — I haven't heard from you in ages! Call me!!!! E.T.

THE COSMIC CASTING COMPANY
The greatest movie stars in the galaxy!

Ready Reference... page 87

And finally, to make sure that you can really make contact with the facts when you need them, there's a Glossary and, of course, an Index.

Jacqueline Mitton

About The Authors

Jacqueline Mitton started sky-watching at a very early age — for one thing, it was a good excuse for staying up late! Since training as an astronomer, she's spotted countless lights glowing and flashing at night, but so far they've all turned out to be natural objects like stars, planets, and meteors. She hasn't met any aliens yet, and doesn't really expect to, but she still thinks our Universe is awesome, and likes to spend her time writing and talking about it.

Michael Johnstone's interest in science fiction was kindled at children's movie matinees, as he watched film stars saving the Earth from alien attack over and over again. Since then he's read lots of books and seen dozens of movies about visitors from outer space. And although he's never actually met any aliens, there have been times at rock concerts when he thought he had! When he's not writing children's books, he's either at the movies or out in the country walking his dog.

BEYOND BELIEF

UFOs

SPECIAL EDITION

THE MAGAZINE WITH ALL THE ANSWERS

Are ALIENS invading the Earth?

In this issue . . .

Letter from the EDITOR

Everyone knows someone who's seen a UFO — a friend who spotted a weird light streaking across the sky one night, or a relative who saw a strange glowing shape hovering near the horizon!

But UFOs aren't necessarily alien spaceships. The letters stand for Unidentified Flying Object, which is just another way of saying "something in the sky that you can't name or explain."

In this special edition of *Beyond Belief* magazine we bring you stories and special features about some of the most dramatic UFO sightings ever reported — plus a range of possible explanations for what people claim to have witnessed.

Read on — and decide for yourself whether UFOs really are out of this world!

" Can't name it . . . can't explain it. "

Pilot puzzled by flock of FLYING objects

USA 1947

American Kenneth Arnold's UFO sighting makes headline news around the world.

On the afternoon of June 24, 1947, businessman Kenneth Arnold was flying his private plane over Washington State's Cascade Mountains, when he spotted nine very shiny objects traveling at tremendous speed in a V-shaped formation. It was a bright sunny day, and the objects were flying above the mountaintops and glinting brilliantly in the sunlight.

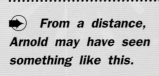

➡ **From a distance, Arnold may have seen something like this.**

Kenneth Arnold, photographed beside his plane in 1947.

Talking to reporters afterward, Mr. Arnold said that he thought the objects were military aircraft until he noticed their strange shape — tailless, and with sweptback wings, like a boomerang.

Even more peculiar was the swooping motion of their flight. "They flew like a saucer would if you skipped it across the water," he said.

In the news report that followed, the mysterious objects were simply described as "saucer-like." Yet within days, sightings were flooding in of

" They Flew like a saucer would . . . "

Arnold described his UFOs as boomerang-shaped. This is how one artist has imagined them.

FACT OR FANTASY

Did Arnold really see UFOs — or was he misled by a flock of birds?

THE EVIDENCE

* Swooping, uneven flight.
* Several objects flying in formation.
* Highflying, light-colored birds can reflect so much sunlight that they can look metallic from far away.
* Arnold himself said that the objects' flight pattern looked similar to that of a flock of geese.

UFOs that didn't just fly like saucers, but looked like them!

Geese flying in formation.

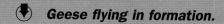

EDITOR'S NOTE:
Arnold's was not the first-ever UFO sighting. People had been reporting strange lights and shapes in the sky for hundreds of years. But the year 1947 marked the start of sightings of disc- or saucer-shaped UFOs. It was also the first time the term "flying saucer" was ever used.

FLYING SAUCER
crashes in Roswell region!

USA 1947

> Rancher William "Mac" Brazel discovers weird wreckage on his New Mexico property.

There had been a violent storm during the night of July 2, 1947, but one of the noises heard by Brazel had sounded more like an explosion than thunder.

The next day he discovered wreckage made from materials he'd never seen before, including a foil-like metal which couldn't be cut or burned.

Brazel got in touch with the US Army's air base at nearby Roswell. Military personnel then removed the wreckage and closed the site to the public.

Hundreds of "flying saucer" sightings had been reported since the Kenneth Arnold incident a few weeks earlier, and the military were quick to issue this statement: "The many rumors regarding

> " Metal which couldn't be cut or burned. "

FACT OR FANTASY

There is no doubt today that the information given out by US military officials in 1947 was misleading, and that an attempt was made to cover up something.

The typical flying saucer of the 1940s and 1950s looked like a car hubcap or an upturned soup dish.

flying discs became a reality yesterday." But within hours they said they'd made a mistake. Pieces of a weather balloon were shown at a press conference, and journalists were told that this was the wreckage discovered by Brazel.

In 1997 the US military issued a report saying that the wreckage came from a top-secret experiment. This involved dropping humanlike dummies by parachute, to test ways for pilots to escape from planes flying as high as 100,000 feet above the ground. We can't be certain that this is the truth either, but it is quite likely that what Brazel found was wreckage from some sort of secret military experiment that went wrong.

In 1947 the US military showed the wreckage to the press, claiming it was from a weather balloon.

THE EVIDENCE

✱ There are several top-secret military research establishments near Roswell, including the White Sands Proving Grounds, where rockets and missiles are tested.

Man meets ALIEN

USA 1952

American travels to the Moon and the planets with blond-haired, green-eyed Venusian!

Sixty-one-year-old UFO enthusiast George Adamski claims that on November 20, 1952, he saw a flying saucer leave a cigar-shaped UFO and land in California's Mojave Desert.

When he got closer to the landing site, Adamski was approached by a young "man" with gray-green eyes and long blond hair, dressed in a brown one-piece suit. The "man" then used sign

Adamski claimed not only to have seen UFOs, he said he had photographed them. Experts say the photos are fakes!

language and telepathy ("speaking" mind to mind) to tell Adamski he was from the planet Venus.

More meetings followed, during which Adamski's alien friend took him on trips to the far side of the Moon and to Venus and other planets.

Adamski, who worked at a café near the Palomar Observatory, was the first person to claim seriously that he had met an extraterrestrial being.

FACT OR FANTASY

Back in the 1950s, astronomers knew very little about the conditions on Venus, or any of the other planets besides Earth. Here's what we know about Venus and the Moon today — was Adamski telling the truth?

THE EVIDENCE

✹ Venus has a poisonous atmosphere made mainly of carbon dioxide gas, and its temperature reaches as high as 900°F — hot enough to melt lead. No human-like beings could live or evolve there.

✹ Adamski claimed to have seen rivers and trees on the Moon, whereas we know that it is rocky and barren.

⬆ *Adamski claimed this photograph showed a Venusian mother ship surrounded by smaller UFOs.*

AN ALIEN

SPECIAL FEATURE

Although people who claim to have seen aliens have described many different types, extraterrestrial beings are mostly reported as looking "humanoid" — walking upright on two legs, with two arms, a head, and a recognizable face.

THE GRAYS ➡

Supposed sightings of this kind of alien began to be reported during the 1950s, in the United States. Nowadays the Grays are the most popular image people have of aliens.

Height	About 5 feet
Distinguishing features	Bald head, with large oval eyes and grayish skin (its nickname comes from its skin color).

GRAB BAG

THE SNOWMEN ➨

A Spanish farmer claims to have seen these aliens near the village of Turis in 1979.

Height	About 3 feet
Distinguishing features	Strange sticking-out glasses, but rest of face blank. Head and most of body covered by shiny white overalls. Feet looked like boxing gloves.

⬅ THE TROLL

T wo Finns reported meeting this alien when they were skiing at Imjärvi in 1970.

Height	Under 3 feet
Distinguishing features	Very thin, with hooked nose and pointed ears. Wearing cone-shaped metal helmet.

THE ELEPHANT MEN ➨

T wo Americans say they saw these aliens in 1973 near the Pascagoula River, Mississippi.

Height	5 feet
Distinguishing features	Wrinkled, elephantlike skin, trunklike legs, and arms ending in pincers. Pointed, rodlike nose and ears.

THE MEN

SPECIAL FEATURE

As if seeing a UFO isn't frightening enough, some witnesses claim that what happens afterward can be even scarier!

R umors about Men in Black (MIB) started circulating back in the 1950s, when a few UFO witnesses began claiming that after reporting their sighting they were harassed by sinister, dark-suited strangers.

SECRET AGENTS?

In some stories, the MIB claim to be from a secret government agency, set up to hide the fact that aliens have landed on Earth. In others, the MIB are themselves aliens — trying to do the same thing!

IN BLACK

In a typical MIB story, two dark-suited men turn up at the UFO witnesses' home. The MIB grill the witnesses about their sighting and try to remove any evidence. The witnesses are told to forget about their sighting — and warned never to tell anyone about the MIB's visit.

COVERING UP?

Such stories continue to this day, mainly in Britain and the USA, but there's never been any evidence to prove that Men in Black exist.
No one knows quite what causes the stories. Perhaps it's because some people are suspicious of their government and believe that information about aliens would be kept secret. Events like the Roswell incident of 1947, where officials were shown to have given out misleading information, might give rise to this kind of distrust.

← *Agents Jay (left, Will Smith) and Kay (right, Tommy Lee Jones), the stars of the 1997 movie* Men in Black.

HAVE A CLOSE

SPECIAL FEATURE

It was a professor of astronomy, Dr. J. Allen Hynek, who invented the term "close encounters of the third kind," used by Steven Spielberg as the title for his 1977 movie. Hynek defined three kinds of close encounters in his book *The UFO Experience: a scientific inquiry* (published in 1972). Two further kinds have since been added.

1 Close encounter of the first kind: a close-up sighting of a UFO.

2 Close encounter of the second kind: physical evidence of the UFO is left behind (such as traces of its landing), or the UFO has a physical effect either on objects, or on humans or other animals.

◄ *A close encounter of the first kind from the 1982 movie E.T.*

ENCOUNTER!

3 Close encounter of the third kind: aliens are sighted.

4 Close encounter of the fourth kind: humans are abducted by aliens.

5 Close encounter of the fifth kind: humans make contact with aliens (communicating through signals or telepathy).

➡ *Picking up an alien radio signal, a close encounter of the fifth kind from the 1997 movie* Contact.

⬅ *As well as being an astronomer, Hynek was one of the world's most respected UFO investigators.*

19

MYSTERY light sparks UFO chase

Witnesses spot speeding UFO over the Australian town of Kempsey!

Australia 1975

It was about 8 P.M. on July 21, 1975, and a couple were driving westward out of town. Suddenly, they saw a large bright light in the sky. They chased the light, which seemed to be moving even faster than a jet plane, and then stopped their car to watch it.

"Moving even faster than a jet plane"

The UFO slowed and then appeared to hover just above the horizon for about 10 minutes, changing color from white to yellow to red. Finally it dropped out of sight behind the hills.

*The witnesses
watched the light
hovering above
the horizon.*

FACT OR FANTASY

Many reported UFO
sightings are actually of natural
space objects such as planets. Earth's
atmosphere also creates many bewildering
effects — some of them dramatically
beautiful, and others, distinctly creepy.
Sometimes, either planets or these
atmospheric effects are mistaken for UFOs.

THE EVIDENCE

✴ The planet Venus is the next brightest
object in the sky after the Sun and the
Moon, and it can look amazingly brilliant.
Stars and planets set in the west, as the
Sun does, and very bright ones can be
mistaken for UFOs as they sink toward
the horizon.

*Three of the brightest planets visible
in our night sky — Venus, Mars, and
Jupiter (from left to right).*

FACT OR FANTASY

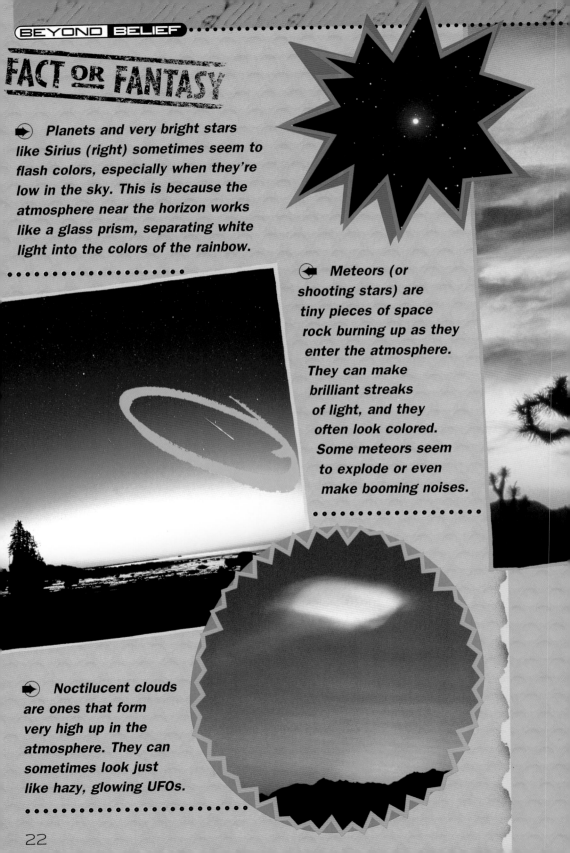

➡ Planets and very bright stars like Sirius (right) sometimes seem to flash colors, especially when they're low in the sky. This is because the atmosphere near the horizon works like a glass prism, separating white light into the colors of the rainbow.

⬅ Meteors (or shooting stars) are tiny pieces of space rock burning up as they enter the atmosphere. They can make brilliant streaks of light, and they often look colored. Some meteors seem to explode or even make booming noises.

➡ Noctilucent clouds are ones that form very high up in the atmosphere. They can sometimes look just like hazy, glowing UFOs.

⬆ ➡ **Lenticular clouds form near mountains and they can look astonishingly like UFOs, too. Sometimes they're shaped like cigars, and at other times like flying saucers.**

➡ *An artist's idea of what a huge triangular-shaped UFO might look like.*

Belgium 1989 • • • •

TRIANGULAR UFOs buzz Belgium

More than 120 witnesses see the same UFO in just one night.

On November 29, 1989, more than a hundred people reported seeing a dark, triangular object with bright lights at each corner. It was huge — some witnesses said it was as big as a soccer field — and moved very slowly, making a faint humming noise. During the following weeks there were so many additional sightings of the mysterious triangular object that in March 1990 a special four-day UFO watch was set up, with official help from the Belgian authorities. Even so, no one managed to track down a real UFO! ➤

FACT OR FANTASY

Since the early 1980s, people the world over have been more likely to report seeing triangular-shaped UFOs than the traditional flying saucers. But how many of these sightings are really of more familiar flying objects — aircraft?

THE EVIDENCE

✸ The US Air Force's F-117A *Nighthawk* first flew in 1981. This plane's triangular shape helps to make it almost invisible to radar, but it is possible to see it with the naked eye.

✸ Aircraft have colored navigation lights, and bright searchlights which are switched on as they come in to land at night. These can create weird effects, and planes are often mistaken for UFOs.

⬅ *The distinctive shape of the F-117A Nighthawk.*

⬇ *Light trails created by an aircraft landing just after sunset.*

Bright LIGHTS cause UFO scare

Britain 1997

A flood of UFO sightings are reported in the British town of Stoke-on-Trent.

On the night of June 2, 1997, no fewer than seven people reported seeing the same UFO. Among them was a young woman who saw it while she was driving home. This is how she described her sighting: "There was a bright light in the sky. It seemed to drift sideways before disappearing into a gap in the clouds."

EDITOR'S NOTE: UFO investigators say the lights were from a spacecraft — but it wasn't being flown by aliens! Sunlight was glinting off the Mir space station, which was over Britain at the time of the sightings.

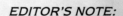 **The narrow streak of light is the path of the Mir space station.**

FACT OR FANTASY

There are several thousand objects in orbit around the Earth — from the International Space Station to all sorts of weather, navigation, or communications satellites, as well as countless pieces of space junk (old rockets and satellites). Sometimes, these are mistaken for UFOs.

THE EVIDENCE

✳ Sometimes a piece of space junk falls out of orbit and turns into a ball of fire as it re-enters the atmosphere.

Burning space junk usually moves more slowly and is more brightly colored than a meteor.

✳ Satellites can often be seen as bright lights gliding across the sky on dark clear nights. Although the Sun is below the horizon, its light sometimes reflects off them, and they may give off either a steady light or a flashing one.

A communications satellite in orbit above Earth.

The last WORD

So, do you still believe UFOs are alien spaceships? It would be immensely exciting if they were, wouldn't it — and just a bit scary!

But although hundreds of UFO sightings are reported every year, the explanations for these mysterious goings-on don't have to be fleets of invading extraterrestrials.

As many as 99 percent of all sightings turn out to be things like meteors, or clouds, or aircraft. And as for the remaining 1 percent that can't be explained — well, there's still a lot that even scientists don't understand about the way our world works.

One thing we are sure of is that there's no scientific proof that aliens have visited our planet . . .

(YET!)

BEYOND BELIEF magazine © Candlewick Press

SPACE CADET SCHOOL

ENTRANCE
EXAMINATION

★★★★★★★★★★★★★★★★★★★★★★★★★★★★★★★★★★★

LOOK TO THE FUTURE —
BE A PART OF THE SEARCH FOR ALIEN LIFE!

SPACE CADET SCHOOL

Affix passport photograph

NAME: Stella Stargazer

DATE OF BIRTH: June 11, 1985

ADDRESS: 34 Star Street, Newtown

CONFIDENTIAL MEMO

TO: Sally Saturnine, DIRECTOR OF STUDIES

FROM: Jim Mooney, ADMISSIONS OFFICER

Stella Stargazer's examination paper is an excellent piece of work — her replies are thorough and very clearly expressed. I've written a few comments (including things I'd like to discuss further if we call her in for an interview). But I'll wait to hear what you think before calling her to arrange a time.

Jim M.

🪐 **Do you think there could be life in the Universe anywhere other than on Earth?**

YES	NO	✓ NOT SURE

★ ★

The Universe is so enormous, it seems quite possible to me that there must be some other form of life out there somewhere.

But although lots of people claim to have seen UFOs (or alien spaceships), there is no scientific proof at all that extraterrestrials have ever visited Earth, or that they even exist!

Compared to all the stars in the Universe, the few we see from Earth are like a handful of sand on a beach!

🪐 In science-fiction stories and movies, aliens are usually pictured as intelligent beings who use a high level of technology. If extraterrestrials exist, do you think they might be like this?

| ☐ YES | ☐ NO | ☑ NOT SURE |

★ ★

These sorts of books and movies are just fantasies. In reality, an extraterrestrial could be any form of life that exists anywhere beyond our planet.

This could include beings that are intelligent but haven't developed technology, or very simple creatures such as bacteria — or even plants!

Dolphins are intelligent, but unlike humans, they haven't developed technology.

GOOD POINT! Would like to discuss the idea further with her. Jim M.

32

🪐 **Do you think life might exist anywhere else in our solar system besides Earth?**

☐ YES   ☐ NO   ☑ NOT SURE

★ ★

Well, no one's found any sign of living creatures yet, and the solar system's been explored fairly thoroughly now. Unmanned spacecraft have sent back close-up pictures of all the planets except Pluto, and probes have even landed on Mars and Venus.

But even though it's not very likely, it is just possible that a tiny life form, such as bacteria, could still be found somewhere in our solar system.

In the year 2004 the *Cassini* spacecraft will reach Saturn and release the Huygens probe toward Titan, the largest of Saturn's 18 moons.

🪐 **What, in your opinion, makes life on Earth possible? How might our understanding of this help us to discover extraterrestrial life forms? Please number your points.**

★ ★

I think there are three main reasons why living things are able to exist on Earth.

Earth has plenty of liquid water — oceans full!

1) LIQUID WATER

Water is really, really important. Even though there are so many different kinds of animals and plants on Earth, they all need water to survive. In fact, virtually all living things (and that includes us humans) are made mostly of water!

2) DISTANCE FROM THE SUN

Earth is 93 million miles away from the Sun — not so near that we get too hot, and not so far away that we get too cold. Our distance from the Sun means that the average temperature on our planet is 72°F. (The Earth's atmosphere also helps with this, though — see my point 3.)

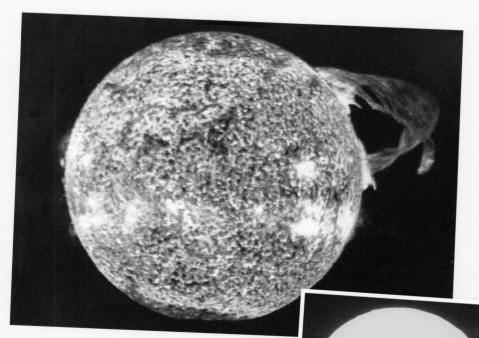

The Sun is a ball of glowing gases (nearly) a hundred times larger in diameter than Earth. It's like a huge power station pouring light and heat energy into space.

It's just over a hundred times bigger, in fact. Jim M.

35

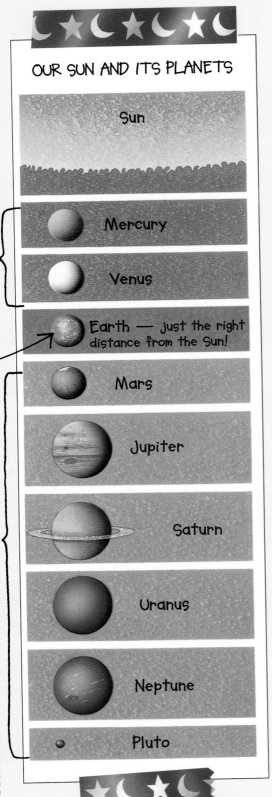

OUR SUN AND ITS PLANETS

Sun

Mercury

Venus

Earth — just the right distance from the Sun!

Mars

Jupiter

Saturn

Uranus

Neptune

Pluto

Too close to the Sun

LIFE ZONE

Too far from the Sun

Earth's temperature is just right for life — warm enough to stop most water from freezing, but not so hot that it all boils away. And as I've just said, life wouldn't survive without liquid water.

We're in what astronomers call the Sun's "life zone" — we're just the right distance from the Sun for there to be liquid water, and therefore, for life as we know it to be possible.

Great diagram, but check she realizes the planets aren't in scale to one another! Jim M.

3) THE ATMOSPHERE

Life on Earth wouldn't exist if we were outside the Sun's life zone. But being in the zone isn't enough on its own — the atmosphere that surrounds our planet is also vital. There are two main reasons for this.

a) The atmosphere helps control Earth's temperature. It acts like a barrier, blocking out some of the Sun's heat so we don't get too hot. And it also works like a blanket, keeping some warmth in so we don't get too cold.

The atmosphere also helps to block the Sun's harmful rays, like the ultraviolet light that can cause skin cancers. Some rays get through, though, so it's important to protect your skin!

The "other gases" include carbon dioxide. This gas makes up 0.03% of the atmosphere.

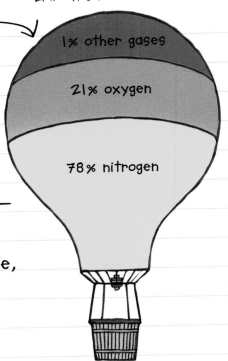

1% other gases

21% oxygen

78% nitrogen

b) The atmosphere also contains important gases — few animals could survive without oxygen, for example, while most plants would die without carbon dioxide.

HOW KNOWING ABOUT ALL THIS MIGHT HELP US TO DISCOVER EXTRATERRESTRIAL LIFE FORMS

Knowing about the Sun's life zone could help us to find extraterrestrials. That's because astronomers think that if there are life forms beyond our solar system, we're most likely to find them on the planets or moons in another star's life zone.

🪐 **The Moon, Venus, and Mars are Earth's nearest neighbors. Why doesn't life exist on them?**

★ ★

1) THE MOON

Although it's in the life zone and there is some frozen water in the rocks near its poles, the Moon doesn't have liquid water or an atmosphere. Everything in the Universe has gravity, and the more massive something is, the stronger its gravity. The Moon is only a quarter of Earth's size, and its gravity is too weak to hold on to an atmosphere.

Astronauts first walked on the Moon in July 1969. So far, the Moon is the farthest that humans have traveled into space.

2) VENUS

Venus is almost the same size as Earth, and it does have an atmosphere. The problem with Venus is that it's too near the Sun to be in the life zone, and it has the wrong kind of atmosphere. Earth's atmosphere has a lot of oxygen gas, but Venus's is mostly carbon dioxide gas. The carbon dioxide traps too much of the Sun's heat, and Venus is so hot (the temperature reaches a scorching 900° F) that any liquid water would just boil away.

Soviet *Venera* probes landed on Venus in 1975, 1978, and 1982. They sent back information and photographs, before being destroyed by the planet's lethal atmosphere.

3) MARS

Mars is only about half Earth's size, but it also has an atmosphere. Like Venus's atmosphere, it's mainly made up of carbon dioxide gas — but there's a lot less of it, so it traps less of the Sun's heat.

Northern icecap

People often call Mars "the Red Planet."

Because of this, and because Mars is so far away from the Sun — much farther than Venus or Earth, of course — temperatures there hardly ever rise above freezing point, even in summer.

TRUE — in fact, the temperature on Mars can drop to as low as −185°F! Jim M.

Various spacecraft have been sent to study Mars — some have even landed probes on its surface. They found a little water vapor in the Martian atmosphere, and a thin layer of frozen water in the icecap at its north pole.

But the spacecraft didn't find living things — Mars just doesn't have enough water to support life as we know it.

In 1997, the tiny Sojourner robot tested rock and soil samples on Mars's surface.

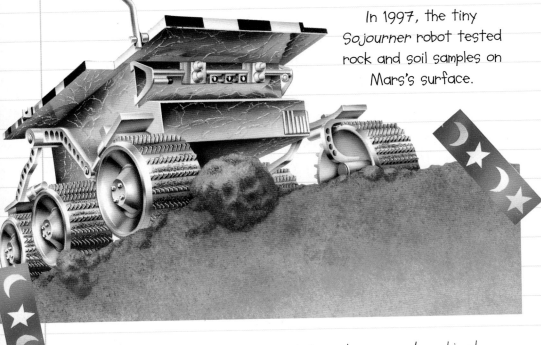

DISCUSS AT INTERVIEW? Although Mars has little water now, it has valleys where huge rivers flowed billions of years ago. Simple life forms may have developed then — but the only way we'll prove this is if we find fossils on Mars.   Jim M.

🪐 **The Universe is so big that looking for signs of life outside our solar system would be like hunting for a needle in a haystack. Is there any way astronomers can work out which stars are most likely to have planets or moons that could support life?**

☑ YES   ☐ NO   ☐ NOT SURE

★ ★

By concentrating on similar stars to our Sun, astronomers think they have a much better chance of finding planets or moons with life on them. Stars are grouped by size, brightness, and temperature. Massive stars are very hot and bright, and most small stars are dim and cool. Our Sun is a medium-sized, medium-hot yellow star.

There are billions of stars in a galaxy, and billions of galaxies in the Universe. This is a photograph of the spiral galaxy known as NCG 2997.

SMALL COOL STARS

Because small cool stars give off less heat
than our Sun, the life zone around them is very
close to the star — and so narrow that the odds
are there won't be a planet in it.

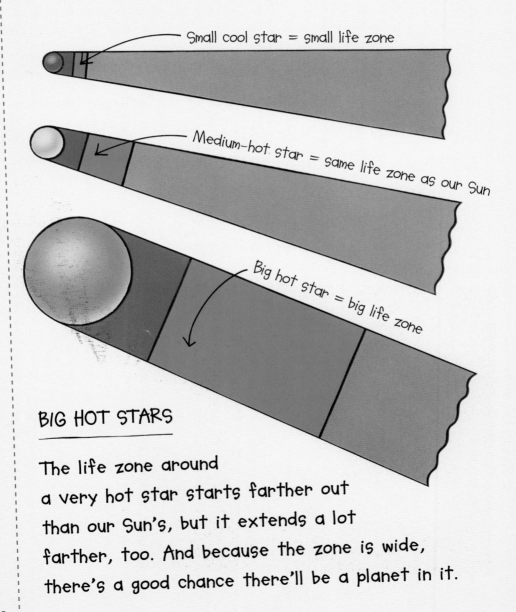

Small cool star = small life zone

Medium-hot star = same life zone as our Sun

Big hot star = big life zone

BIG HOT STARS

The life zone around
a very hot star starts farther out
than our Sun's, but it extends a lot
farther, too. And because the zone is wide,
there's a good chance there'll be a planet in it.

But stars don't shine forever — eventually they run out of energy and die. And the hotter and more massive a star is, the shorter its life.

This picture shows a massive star that's blasting off vast clouds of gas and dust as it starts to die. Eventually it will blow apart in the kind of explosion astronomers call a supernova.

Our Sun is about 5 billion years old, and the first living things probably began to form in Earth's oceans about 3.8 billion years ago.

A star several times the size of the Sun would only last about a billion years. Going by what happened on Earth, that would be far too short a time for even the simplest life forms to develop.

YES — massive stars are too young and short-lived. Jim M.

🪐 **Have astronomers found any stars other than the Sun that have planets? If so, how did they do it?**

✓ YES ☐ NO ☐ NOT SURE

★ ★

YES! Astronomers told us about finding the first one in October 1995, and about three more, early in 1996. All the stars are similar in size, brightness, temperature, and age to our Sun. And more stars with planets have been found since!

One of the nearest new planets belongs to a star called 47 Ursae Majoris, in the constellation Ursa Major (the Great Bear).

Up until 1995, astronomers were only guessing that stars other than the Sun would have planets, but now we know for sure that our solar system isn't the only one in the Universe!

It's about 35 light-years away. Jim M.

46

GEOFF MARCY

PAUL BUTLER

Most of the new planets were discovered by two American astronomers, Geoff Marcy and Paul Butler.

HOW THE ASTRONOMERS DID IT

Even the biggest telescopes aren't powerful enough to pick out planets orbiting other stars, so people have had to come up with a different way of finding them.

What astronomers do is study the light that a star gives out — to see if the star is wobbling. If the star has a regular wobble, this means it's being gently tugged by one or more planets' gravity.

And even though they can't see the planets, astronomers can work out how big each one is by the amount the star wobbles. They even know how long it takes each planet to orbit its star, and how far away the planet is from the star.

GREAT BIG GAS PLANETS

This method can't help us find planets as small as Earth (not yet anyway) because the effect a small planet has on a star is far too tiny for us to detect. So all the planets found so far are pretty massive — like Jupiter and the other giant planets of our own solar system.

The swirling clouds that cover the giant planet Jupiter are made mainly of frozen crystals of ammonia and methane.

Earth Jupiter

Measured across its diameter, Jupiter is 11 times bigger than Earth.

Astronomers think that the new planets are probably made up of gases. If so, they won't have a solid surface where liquid water can flow, and they'll be unlikely to support life as we know it.

But there's a good chance that a star with a giant gas planet will also have smaller, rocky planets like Earth. And giant gas planets might even have rocky moons where some form of life has evolved!

Most of Jupiter's 16 moons are made of rock and ice. This picture shows what Jupiter might look like from the ice-covered surface of one of them, called Europa.

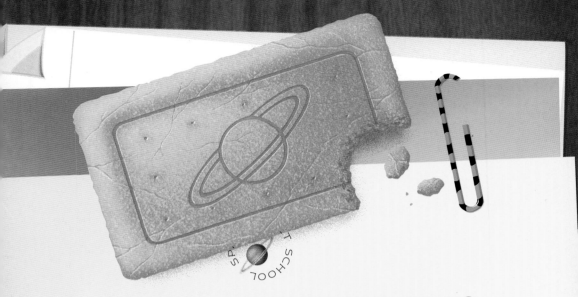

CONFIDENTIAL MEMO

TO: Jim Mooney,
      ADMISSIONS OFFICER

FROM: Sally Saturnine,
       DIRECTOR OF STUDIES

I completely agree with you — it's a
first-rate examination paper. We should
<u>certainly</u> interview Stella Stargazer,
and I think it's very likely we'll be
offering her a place at the school!

Sally

Professor I. M. Wired's

Guide To ExtraTerrestrial Communication

TUNE IN!

The Scientific Search for Alien Radio Signals

Professor I. M. Wired at home with his cats

About the Author

A world-famous expert in extraterrestrial communications, Professor Izzy M. Wired was born in Santa Fe, New Mexico, in 1963. His favorite subject at school was science, and he built his first radio telescope in his backyard when he was 15 years old. After studying engineering and astrophysics in college, he embarked on his brilliant career as a radio astronomer.

In his spare time, Izzy enjoys flying his own plane and writing science-fiction stories. He has homes in Sydney, Australia and Los Angeles, and his closest companions are his wife Wanda and his two cats, Wild and Wicked.

Getting Connected

So you want to talk to an alien? Well, it's not easy, I can tell you, but at least you're starting in the right place — what I don't know about extraterrestrial communication isn't worth knowing!

Making contact

First things first. If you think talking to an alien has anything to do with meeting one, you're in for a big disappointment. No way! If there's one thing we astronomers are sure of it's that there are no — that's N, O — intelligent life forms on any of the other planets in our solar system. (Believe me, I know — I've looked.)

No return

Just take the nearest star to our Sun, Proxima Centauri, for example. It's 25 million million miles away (or 4.2 light-years, as we astronomers would say). If we sent a spaceship there right now, it would be hundreds of thousands of years before it arrived — and any astronauts on it would be nothing more than a pile of dust particles.

Huh!! Are you calling me stupid??!!

Okay, so there might be the odd bacteria lurking out there, but I'm talking about <u>intelligent</u> life forms here. You can't exactly talk to a germ, now can you?

And as for exploring planets beyond our solar system — we can't do that either. Why? Because they're just too far away, that's why.

Wait a minute! How far? How long?

ZOOM

53

Greased lightning

No, the only way to get people to the stars is to travel at close to the speed of light — and at 186,000 miles per second, that's really fast. No one's invented anything yet that comes anywhere near to doing this, but it's not for lack of trying! One team of scientists has even come up with plans for a nuclear-powered rocket that can reach 12 percent of the speed of light. There's just one small problem — they haven't worked out how to stop it!

Of course, even if we <u>humans</u> haven't discovered the secrets of interstellar travel yet, it's always possible that there's a bunch of brainy extraterrestrials out there who have. But unless they drop by and tell us, we'll never know!

Hmm — good, but not quite good enough!

12% of the speed of light
= 186,000 mi/sec ÷ 100 x 12
= 22,320 mi/sec
= PRETTY FAST

The good news

Okay, so you won't be taking an alien home to meet your mother. But there are <u>other</u> ways of making contact with aliens, and we already have the technology to do it. It's all about listening for messages...

On the Right Wavelength

Making waves

Now I'm not talking about any old messages here. I'm talking about ones that will travel through space — the sort of thing that might be sent to and from spacecraft, for example. And that's where radio waves come in.

Why radio waves? Well, they're a kind of energy, like light waves. They even travel at the same speed as light — and we all know there's nothing in the Universe that's any faster.

But there are some things radio waves can do that light waves can't. Light waves get blocked by things like clouds, for example, and believe me, space is littered with clouds of gas and dust!

These space clouds stop light waves dead in their tracks, but radio waves just zap right through them.

Hitching a ride

Take my word for it, there's nothing better than radio waves for sending messages through space. But how is it done?

Well, what happens is that messages are turned into a code and added to radio waves — the messages literally hitch a ride on the radio waves! A radio wave that carries a message is called a <u>carrier wave</u>, and the whole thing — wave and message — is a <u>radio signal</u>.

> Radio waves can travel through me, too!

Are You Receiving Me?

So that's how messages are sent through space. But how exactly do astronomers pick them up? With a telescope, of course! Not the sort you look at the stars through — they're optical telescopes. No, what we use are <u>radio</u> telescopes.

Quite a dish

Optical telescopes pick up light waves, so what do radio telescopes do? You've got it — they pick up radio waves (and, of course, radio signals).

Most radio astronomers use their telescopes to study radio waves from natural objects like stars — only a few of us actually listen for messages from aliens!

Two-way radio

A lot of radio telescopes look a bit like the kind of thing you might use for picking up satellite TV — but a whole lot bigger. However, unlike a TV satellite dish, radio telescopes don't just pick up radio signals — they can also be used to send them.

Let's start with the receiving end. Radio waves are collected by the telescope's dish (1) and then focused onto the feed antenna (2).

1 COLLECTING

The radio waves hit the dish.

2 FOCUSING

The radio waves bounce off the curved sides of the dish toward the feed antenna.

From here, they're directed to a piece of equipment called a receiver (3), and then to a computer. If you're looking at a natural object like a star, the computer turns the radio waves into a radio picture. But if you're hunting for alien radio signals, it scans through the waves, searching for the patterns that might come from an artificial signal.

If you want to use the telescope to send a signal (4), the whole thing just works in reverse. Your signal is directed toward the dish by a piece of equipment called a transmitter. The dish then beams it out into space.

3 <u>RECEIVING</u>

From the feed antenna, the radio waves go to a receiver, and then to a computer which analyzes the data.

Pretty smart, huh?

4 SENDING MESSAGES

A transmitter sends the radio signal down to the dish, which beams it out into space.

57

Feeling faint?

There is one problem with radio waves — the farther they travel, the fainter they get, and the harder they are to pick up. We astronomers have an answer for this, though. We just use bigger and more powerful telescopes.

⬆ This big radio telescope is at Parkes, Australia. Its dish measures 210 feet in diameter.

⬆ This is the world's largest radio telescope. It's at a place called Arecibo, and its dish antenna measures 1,000 feet across — that's as long as three soccer fields!

Arecibo is on the Caribbean island of Puerto Rico — great place for a vacation!

Spot the difference

So that's enough about how radio telescopes work. Let's get back to talking to aliens.

Suppose an alien wants to send a message to us. The first thing we have to do is find its radio signals — and that's like looking for one grain of sand on a beach!

The problem is, space is flooded with natural radio waves — they're given out by the Sun and other stars, even by gas clouds between the stars.

So with all these natural radio waves buzzing about, what we need is a way of picking out the ones that carry messages — the radio signals. Luckily for us, there's a basic difference between <u>natural</u> radio waves and <u>artificial</u> radio signals.

Tuning in

Think about the signals you pick up on your radio at home. Say your favorite radio station broadcasts on 95.8. You can't pick the station up if you tune your radio a bit too high or low — you have to hit 95.8 right on the nail. That's because each radio station broadcasts on a particular frequency. Frequency is measured in hertz, kilohertz, and megahertz — and 95.8 is really a frequency of 95.8 megahertz.

RADIO FREQUENCY

The word <u>frequency</u> means "how often something happens," and <u>radio frequency</u> tells you the rate at which radio waves or signals are given out. It's measured in hertz, kilohertz, and megahertz:

- 1 hertz (Hz) = 1 wave per second
- 1 kilohertz (kHz) = 1,000 waves per second
- 1 megahertz (MHz) = 1,000,000 waves per second

Needle in a haystack

You're probably wondering what frequency's got to do with the difference between natural radio waves and artificial radio signals.

Well, radio stations broadcast their signals on a <u>specific</u> frequency — 95.8 megahertz, for example. This kind of broadcasting is called a narrowband emission — and <u>emission</u> is just another way of saying "giving out."

Natural objects like the Sun, on the other hand, give out radio waves over a <u>wide range</u> of frequencies all at once. This is known as a broad-band emission.

So, the good news is that all we have to do if we're to find artificial radio signals is to hunt for a narrow-band emission. The bad news is that there are billions of frequencies out in space to search through.

This hasn't stopped people from trying, though — we astronomers don't give up that easily!

60

The Search Begins

The first time a radio telescope was officially used to hunt for alien radio signals was about 40 years ago — on April 8, 1960, to be exact.

Blast off

A radio astronomer called Frank Drake had talked some of his colleagues at the US National Radio Astronomy Observatory in West Virginia into aiming a telescope at a couple of stars called Tau Ceti and Epsilon Eridani.

Drake had chosen these two stars because they're similar in size, age, and temperature to our Sun — and Sun-like stars are the ones most likely to have planets where life may have developed. The stars are also fairly close to us — in space terms, anyway. They're actually 11 light-years away!

Tau Ceti and Epsilon Eridani were monitored for a total of 200 hours over three months. Drake's team didn't pick up any alien messages, but then they'd sampled only a tiny fraction of all the possible frequencies, and just two out of a galaxy of stars!

Somewhere over the rainbow . . .

Wizard of Oz

Drake called his experiment Project Ozma after the children's story, <u>Ozma of Oz</u>. He'd loved it as a child and said that like the author he was "dreaming of a land far away, peopled by strange and exotic beings."

The author was L. Frank Baum, by the way, and if his book title sounds familiar, it's probably because you've seen the film <u>The Wizard of Oz</u>, which was based on one of his other stories!

Get ready, get SETI

Project Ozma was only the beginning, though. Radio astronomers have carried out more than 70 search projects since then, using radio telescopes all over the world. This branch of radio astronomy has become known as SETI, which stands for the Search for ExtraTerrestrial Intelligence.

The biggest SETI project ever began in the early 1990s and is still going on today. Called Project Phoenix, it's monitoring about 1,000 stars within 200 light-years of the Sun.

This is no easy task. As I said before, there are literally billions of frequencies out there, and aliens might be broadcasting a message on any one of them. Can you imagine how long it would take to check through billions of frequencies one at a time, for each and every single star?

It sounds impossible, doesn't it! Radio engineers have come up with an answer, though. Over the years, they've developed extremely powerful radio receivers that can monitor <u>tens of millions</u> of frequencies all at once.

Brain strain

These receivers produce a mindboggling amount of data. But the job of sifting through it is done by more machines — supercomputers programmed to hunt for unusual radio signals.

Machines can't do all the work, of course. If the computers do find anything, it still takes a human astronomer to work out whether the signal is a real message from an alien civilization or just a false alarm.

So far we've had only false alarms, but who knows — tomorrow might just be our lucky day!

To Boldly Go ...

We aren't just listening for messages from aliens — we're also bombarding them with our own. Few of the messages are being sent on purpose, though!

Junk mail

In fact, most of these messages are radio and TV shows — the ones you and I tune in to every day.

How come? Well, since the first radio and television stations began broadcasting in the 1920s and '30s, their signals have been flooding out into space as well as into our homes.

In fact, the very first time we intentionally tried to communicate with aliens, it had nothing to do with radio signals — what we did was put the messages on spacecraft!

This is Pioneer 10 — the first interstellar mailbox!

Address unknown

So which spacecraft are we talking about here? Well, when Pioneers 10 and 11 were launched in 1972 and 1973, and Voyagers 1 and 2 in 1977, they were heading toward the outer solar system — and they all carried descriptions of our planet and the people who live on it.

Picture puzzles

Pioneers 10 and 11 are carrying similar engraved plaques. These show a man and a woman standing in front of the spacecraft, along with a diagram of our solar system and the path each spacecraft took from Earth. There's also a kind of star map to help pinpoint our solar system in space.

Easy listening

Voyagers 1 and 2 carry audio and video messages on gold-coated copper discs. Each spacecraft's disc includes 118 photographs showing the solar system and life on Earth, greetings in 60 languages, and different music from around the world. There's also a similar star map to the one on the Pioneer plaques.

This is Pioneer 10's message. Let's hope aliens wave when they're being friendly!

This is **Voyager 1** — the first interstellar VCR!!!

President's present

Jimmy Carter, who was the president of the United States at the time, added a message to the Voyager discs on behalf of us all. This is part of what he said:

"This is a present from a small distant world, a token of our sounds, our science, our images, our music, our thoughts and our feelings. We are attempting to survive our time so we may live into yours. We hope, someday, having solved the problems we face, to join a community of galactic civilizations. This record represents our hope and our determination, and our good will in a vast and awesome Universe."

See you in a few thousand years!

Long-distance travelers

So why were these particular spacecraft chosen to be our messengers rather than any others? Basically, it was because they were the first ones we'd ever sent on such long journeys. Between them they were going to study the four gas giants — Jupiter, Saturn, Uranus, and Neptune — and then leave our solar system and head out toward the stars.

By January 1998, more than twenty years after it was launched from Earth, Voyager 1 had traveled well over 7.5 billion miles, and overtaken Pioneers 10 and 11 to become the most distant human-made object in the Universe.

Voyager 1 is now zipping away from our solar system at the speed of 39,000 miles per hour. It has enough power to stay in touch with Earth until about the year 2020, but after that we'll lose track of it forever.

Late delivery

Don't expect an early reply to any of our messages, though. It'll take the four spacecraft hundreds of thousands of years to reach the stars nearest to Earth. And the only way we'll know if any of them have been found will be if an alien spaceship comes to tell us!

Drake's progress

D: So what were the SETI researchers doing while all this was going on? Well, they were still planning and carrying out search projects for alien radio signals, of course.

But then, on November 16, 1974, something remarkable happened — we sent our first, and so far <u>only</u>, intentional radio signal to aliens.

The message was beamed out from the huge radio telescope at the Arecibo Observatory on the island of Puerto Rico. And the person responsible for sending it was the head of the observatory, Professor Frank Drake — that's right, the same man who'd set up the Project Ozma team back in 1960.

▶ Drake's message included coded diagrams of the telescope's dish, a human figure, and the solar system.

Playing the odds

P: But guess what! There's no point holding your breath for a reply to this message, either.

By the year 2000, the signal had already been traveling out into space at the speed of light for 25 years. At 25 light-years away from Earth, the odds on it having passed any stars with planets around them are very slim. And if by any chance it has, the odds are just about zero that those planets are home to intelligent life forms.

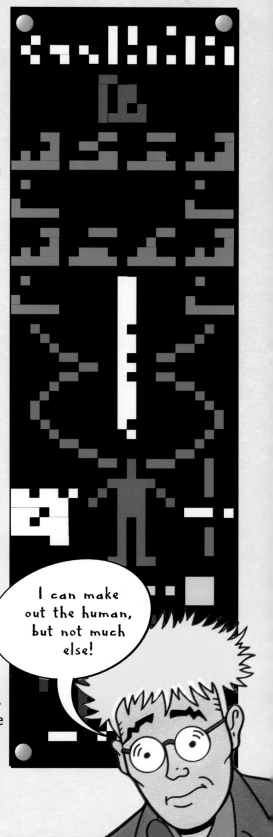

I can make out the human, but not much else!

Getting the Message

Right, so now you know what's being done to contact aliens. But what would happen if aliens got in touch with us?

Shock waves

Say one day some SETI researchers find a signal they can't explain. They check and recheck, and they're sure there's no natural explanation for it. They're certain it's an <u>artificial</u> radio signal containing some kind of message from an alien intelligence. What will happen next?

Friend or foe?

Well, for one thing, everyone's going to be arguing about whether or not we should reply!

Some of us can't wait to make contact with intelligent life forms from another planet. Just think what we might learn from them — the whole idea is mindblowing!

Time travel? You mean you <u>don't know how</u> to do it?

But there are people who think it would be better if we didn't advertise our address across the entire galaxy. What if we replied and the aliens decided to pay us a visit? To do this, they'd have to be able to build the kind of spaceship that would get them here. But if our alien visitors were this smart and were hostile, they might also be capable of wiping out our whole planet!

Ground rules

Whichever way you look at it, picking up an alien signal is going to be one of the most important events in the entire history of the human race. And deciding what to do about it isn't going to be easy.

It's because of this that SETI researchers, along with other scientists, have come up with a document stating how <u>they</u> think we should respond.

In it, they say that the discovery should not be kept secret — everyone should be told. No one should reply to the signal until international meetings have been held to discuss what to do. And if any reply is made, it should be on behalf of the whole human race, not simply the people who find the signal.

Why Are We Waiting?

Of course, there <u>are</u> people who think the reason why we haven't heard anything yet is because extraterrestrials don't exist — but I don't happen to agree with them! There could be lots of explanations for why we're still waiting to hear from aliens. I'll leave you with a few of my favorites:

- Interstellar distances are so vast that, like us, aliens haven't yet found a way to cross them.

- Aliens simply aren't interested in exploring space to look for other civilizations.

- A group of alien worlds has joined forces and formed a galactic club. They've set aside our planet as a kind of zoo. They're leaving us alone, but they're watching to see how we develop. . . .

Never give up hope!

MIKEY
Hiram called — can you put the casting notes in the mail today!

MIKEY — I haven't heard fr
you in ages! Call me!!!! E.T

THE **COSMIC CASTING COMPANY**

The greatest movie stars in the galaxy!

THE COSMIC CASTING COMPANY

Palm Tree Boulevard ◆ Hollywood ◆ USA 34500

Hiram Cheeply
WINSOME FILMS INC.
Titanic House
New York, NY

Dear Hiram,

Many thanks for sending me the script for your new movie <u>Aliens Are Eating Our Cornflakes</u>. I'm thrilled that you've asked C.C.C. to send you casting notes for the aliens on our books.

Here they are — a weirder bunch you're unlikely to meet this side of the Moon! Hope you agree.

Will I see you at Cannes again this year?

All the best,

Mikey

Michael Johnstone
CASTING AGENT

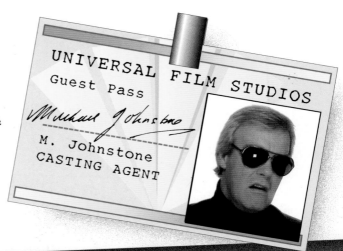

UNIVERSAL FILM STUDIOS
Guest Pass

M. Johnstone
CASTING AGENT

CASTING NOTES NO. 1

THE ALIEN

STAR RATING
10/10

FIRST SEEN? 1979 in the movie classic *Alien*.

WHERE FROM? It's planted inside an astronaut when he leaves the spaceship *Nostromo* to answer another ship's distress signal.

DRAMATIC ENTRANCE? The best! The hungry little alien bursts out of the astronaut's stomach. Then it grows . . . and grows . . . and grows . . .

UNTIL? It's chomped through five of the other astronauts, <u>and</u> given the spaceship's cat a couple of nasty moments.

AND THEN WHAT? It's sucked out into space when the last surviving astronaut opens a hatch. BUT we do have more on our books — the stars of the sequels, *Aliens* (1986), *Alien 3* (1992), and *Alien Resurrection* (1997)!

THE KLINGONS

FIRST SEEN? On the big screen in 1979, in *Star Trek — The Motion Picture*, but they've been in the TV series since 1967.

THE MOTION PICTURE? With Admiral Kirk at the helm, the *Enterprise* saves the Earth from certain destruction at the hands of V'Ger, a massive living machine.

WHERE FROM? Klingons were originally from the planet Qo'noS. They now control a vast space empire and fight for the Federation (on the same side as Kirk and the *Enterprise*).

THEY LOOK A BIT FIERY! They <u>are</u> fiery. Tough, too — great for action movies. Not so good for romantic movies, though. They haven't got any tear ducts, so they can't cry!

STAR RATING 6/10

MING THE MERCILESS

STAR RATING ★ 6/10 ★

FIRST SEEN? In glorious Technicolor in 1980, in the movie *Flash Gordon*. But he first appeared more than 40 years before that, in cartoon strips.

WHERE FROM? He's ruler of the planet Mongo — the girl's his daughter, by the way.

WHO'S SHE STARING AT? None other than Flash Gordon himself — an American football hero who beams up to Mongo and stops Ming from destroying the Earth.

DOES MING SUCCEED? Of course not! In fact, he ends up with the tip of Flash's spacecraft stuck right through his chest.

MING DIES, THEN? No way! As the credits roll, the sound of his mocking laughter tells us he'll be back to fight another day.

HIRAM — watch this guy, and don't let him use the phone! Mikey

STAR RATING 10/10

CASTING NOTES NO. 4

E.T.

FIRST SEEN? 1982 in the hit movie *E.T.*

E.T? He's an extraterrestrial — from out there, somewhere.

HOW DOES HE GET HERE? He's with a party of other E.T.s who land to see what Earth's like. They're spotted, though, and chased back to their spaceship. Sadly, this little E.T. doesn't make it in time.

STILL HERE? No! He made friends with a couple of kids who helped him get home.

GOOD PERFORMER? There's a saying among actors: "Never appear with children or animals." Add E.T. to the list. He walks (and cycles) away with the movie!

DRAWBACKS? He can't pass a phone without trying to call home.

ANY SPECIAL TRICKS? Besides making his fingertips glow, you mean? Well, he has a winning way with droopy plants and can turn an ordinary bike ride into a real flight of fantasy!

MOST LIKELY TO SAY? "Can I use your phone, please?"

HATES TO HEAR? The busy signal.

JUST THE ONE MOVIE? Yes, but he's out there somewhere — and he's sure to be waiting for the call.

JABBA THE HUTT

STAR RATING 8/10

FIRST SEEN? 1983 in *Return of the Jedi*, the third of the original three *Star Wars* movies. But when the movies were re-released in 1997, he was given a part in *Star Wars: A New Hope*, the first of the three.

WHERE FROM? He's a kind of invertebrate, and his home planet is called Nal Hutta.

INVERTEBRATE? It means "no backbone."

SO HE'S SPINELESS? Don't let <u>Jabba</u> hear you say that!

OCCUPATION? Successful master criminal — until Princess Leia gets her hands on him, and he chokes to death.

HE'S DEAD? Sure! But this is show business — he could always make a comeback!

BIB FORTUNA

FIRST SEEN? Same movie as his boss, Jabba the Hutt.

WHERE FROM? He's a Twi'lek from the planet Ryloth.

WHAT'S THAT AROUND HIS NECK? His *lekku* — it looks like a hair extension, doesn't it? It's actually a brain extension. All Twi'leks have one.

SO HE'S SMART? Smart enough to be off like a shot when things got too hot at Jabba's headquarters!

NIEN NUNB

FIRST SEEN? He's in the *Return of the Jedi*, too — but with the Alliance, the side opposite Jabba's crowd.

WHERE FROM? His home planet is Sullust.

ANY SPECIAL TALENTS? He's an ace pilot, and he can see in the dark — great for night scenes. And since he can memorize a star chart or a flight plan in seconds, film scripts are a piece of cake.

HIRAM — I can't find these guys' star ratings. I'll e-mail them later. Mikey

THE CREEPS

STAR
4
10
RATING

FIRST SEEN? 1986 in the movie *Night of the Creeps.*

WHERE FROM? The first one's a black sluglike thing which falls to Earth from a spacecraft.

THEN WHAT? It jumps into a boy's mouth and lays its eggs in his brain. Eventually, these hatch into lots of little Creeps.

INFECT OTHERS?
Yes, including a dog and a busload of students.

ANY WEAKNESSES? Fire — Creeps burn as easily as a box of matches in a barbecue.

SO THEY ALL BURN TO DEATH? Yes, apart from the one we have on our books. But if you're planning on using it, make sure you keep your mouth shut on set!

HIRAM — Creeps and Crites are dead scary! Don't watch their movies alone!! Mikey

STAR RATING 4/10

CASTING NOTES NO. 9

THE CRITES

FIRST SEEN? 1986 in the movie *Critters*.

WHERE FROM? They escape from a prison on an asteroid, steal a spaceship, and head for Earth — with two bounty hunters hot on their tails.

ARE THEY CAUGHT? They terrorize a Kansas farmer and his family first, but the bounty hunters get their Crites in the end.

ALL OF THEM? The last one's killed when the farmer's son blows up the stolen spaceship, but . . .

BUT? Three Crite eggs are left in the farmer's chicken coop.

DO THEY HATCH? Just in time to star in the 1988 sequel *Critters 2: The Main Course*, and then in the follow-ups *Critters 3* (1992) and *Critters 4* (1994).

THE CAPTURED ALIEN

FIRST SEEN? In the 1996 blockbuster movie *Independence Day.*

WHERE FROM? Some planet billions of light-years away — the aliens never said what it was called, and I'm not going to ask them!

BIG SHIP! The one above? It's big enough to cover an entire city and wipe it out in seconds!

WHY? Why else? So the aliens can take over the Earth, of course!

THIS ONE GOT CAPTURED? Its spacecraft crashed in the desert, after a dogfight with a US Air Force jet.

DO THE ALIENS SUCCEED IN TAKING OVER? Come on! This is Hollywood!

STAR RATING ★ ★ 7/10

THE MARTIAN AMBASSADOR

FIRST SEEN? His first movie appearance was in 1996 in *Mars Attacks*. But back in 1962 he was featured in a series of chewing gum cards.

WHERE FROM? Think about it!

STAR RATING 8/10

HOW DOES HE GET HERE?

The Martians land flying saucers in the Nevada Desert and say they've come in peace.

HAVE THEY?

You're joking! They zap the reception committee and wipe out the US Congress — and that's just for starters.

WHO WINS? We do, after discovering that country-and-western music literally blows their minds out. Don't cast them in a musical!

CASTING NOTES NO. 12

EDGARBUG

HIRAM — this guy is really bugging me for work! Mikey

◆◆◆◆◆◆◆◆◆◆◆◆◆◆◆◆◆◆◆◆◆◆◆◆◆◆◆◆◆◆◆

FIRST SEEN? In the 1997 smash hit *Men in Black*.

WHERE FROM? The MIB's files don't say where Edgarbug is from, but he's one of their four most-wanted aliens.

HOW DOES HE GET HERE? By spaceship — it crash-lands on a truck. Then he takes over the body of a farmer who comes to see what all the noise is about. He wants to take over the galaxy, too, but the MIB always get their alien.

STAR RATING 9/10

HOW DO THEY DO THAT? In the end he turns back into a giant cockroach, and the MIB blow him to pieces. . . .

ANY MORE OF THEM? Are you kidding? He's a cockroach. Of course there's more of them!

CASTING NOTES No. 13

THE DIVA

FIRST SEEN? In the 1997 movie *The Fifth Element.*

WHERE FROM? She doesn't say which planet. She's an opera singer who sounds like she's got a choir of angels in her throat — which is surprising when you think what she's got in her stomach.

WHAT'S THAT? Four stone columns, which have to be taken to an Egyptian temple to save Earth from being destroyed by the forces of evil.

SO SHE'S A GOOD GUY? Exactly, and Earth is saved again, as well. But make sure you've got a hankie — the Diva does the best death scene in the business.

THE BUGS

STAR ★ 4/10 ★ RATING

FIRST SEEN? In the 1997 movie *Starship Troopers*.

WHERE FROM? They're huge creepy-crawlies that have infested various planets, including Klendathu and Tango Urilla.

ACTION MOVIE? And how! When the Bugs bombard Earth with meteorites, our elite space warriors, the Starship Troopers, take to their spacecraft — and it's battle stations, everyone.

DO THE TROOPERS WIN? It's a long story. All but one of them is killed in the first mission. But then the Troopers make a second raid into space and snatch victory from the jaws of defeat.

SO THE UNIVERSE IS DEBUGGED? Sadly, no! There are more Bugs out there, waiting for the sequel. . . .

GLoSSARY

INDəX

READY REFERENCE

GLOSSARY

EXTRATERRESTRIAL

Extra and terra are Latin words that mean "outside" and "earth," and extraterrestrial means "coming from outside the Earth." It is often shortened to the initials E.T. (ExtraTerrestrial).

GRAVITY

Gravity is the pulling force that keeps the Moon in orbit around our planet, and which tugs us, and everything else on Earth, down to the ground and stops us from flying off into space. Everything in the Universe has gravity — from stars to planets and moons — but the more massive the object, the greater its gravity.

INTERSTELLAR TRAVEL

Interstellar means "between the stars," and interstellar travel is when a spacecraft goes outside our solar system and heads toward another star.

LIFE ZONE

The region around a star in which the temperature is warm enough for water to remain liquid — any closer and it's so hot that water boils away, and any farther away and it's so cold that water freezes. Without liquid water, life would not exist on Earth — the living things on our planet need liquid water to survive. A life zone is therefore a region in which life as we know it is possible.

LIGHT-YEAR

The distance that a beam of light travels in a year — 5,878,767 million miles.

MASS

The mass of an object is the amount of matter, or material, it contains.

SETI

SETI stands for the Search for Extra-Terrestrial Intelligence, and it is used to describe the work done by scientists hunting for extraterrestrial radio messages.

SPEED OF LIGHT

Light travels at a speed of 186,000 miles per second — nothing in the Universe is faster.

UFO

UFO stands for Unidentified Flying Object — something in the sky that you cannot recognize or explain.

INDɛX

Cow Kidnapped in Kansas!

In 1897, farmer Alexander Hamilton claimed his cow had been kidnapped by a cigar-shaped UFO. However, Hamilton later admitted he belonged to a "liars club," whose members competed to tell the biggest lies!

Fake Film

A video that was first screened in 1995 is supposed to show aliens captured at Roswell in 1947. Experts say it's a fake.

LIFE ON MARS?

In 1996, NASA scientists thought they'd found fossilized bacteria on a meteorite that came to Earth from Mars 3,600 million years ago. But other scientists say there aren't any fossils, and that the meteorites were contaminated some time after they landed on Earth.

EARLY RISERS

The first bacteria probably developed 3,800 million years ago. They were among the earliest living things on Earth.

WATER OF LIFE?

Scientists think there may be an ocean of liquid water well outside the Sun's life zone — beneath the icy surface of Jupiter's moon Europa! The heat needed to keep Europa's ocean from freezing may come from Jupiter's gravity tugging the water around (just as Earth's tides are caused by the pull of the Sun and the Moon).

SPACE OASIS

In 1998, a NASA spacecraft found frozen water in rocks near the Moon's poles. The discovery means it will be easier for people to live there one day!

ACKNOWLEDGMENTS

PHOTOGRAPHS

Air Photo Supply: 25m.
AllSport: 37.
Anglo-Australian Observatory: 43.
Mary Evans Picture Library: 8, 10; George Adamski 6, 12, 13; Dennis Stacy 19b.
Galaxy Picture Library: Robin Scagell 26.
The Kobal Collection: Columbia 16–17; Lucas Film/20th Century Fox 78; New Line/SHO/Smart Egg 81; Paramount 74; Universal 71, 76tl, 77br; Warner Bros. 18, 19t.
Geoff Marcy: 47.
NASA: 33, 35m.
NHPA: Bill Coster 9.
Oxford Scientific Films: Howard Hall 32.
The Ronald Grant Archive: Buena Vista 86; Tri-Star Pictures Inc. 80; 20th Century Fox 73, 79, 82, 85; Universal 75, 76–77; Warner Bros. 83.
Science Photo Library: 27b; Chris Butler 65; David Ducros 70; Simon Fraser 22b; David Hardy 63; John Mead 58b; Allan Morton 22tr; NASA 29, 39, 64; David Nunuk 22m, 23t, 25b; David Parker 58t; Dr. Robert Spicer 23b; U.S. Geological Survey 41; Frank Zullo 21, 31 & 35br.
Tony Stone Images: 34.

ILLUSTRATIONS

Richard Adams (at Inkshed)**:** 5, 11.
Beth Aves: 1–4, 27, 67, 88.
Michael Carroll: 49.
Sidney Coldridge (at Folio)**:** 82, 84.
Roger Goode (at Beehive)**:** 42.
Clive Goodyer (at Pennant Illustration)**:** 51, 53–57, 59–63, 66, 68–69.
Robin Heighway-Bury (at Thorogood Illustration)**:** 87, 92.
David Juniper (at Folio)**:** 20–21.
Martin Macrae (at Folio)**:** 5 (inset), 7, 8–9, 14–15, 28.
Luis Rey: 12–13.
Ian Thompson: 24, 29, 36, 38, 40, 44, 45, 48, 50.
Rod Vass (at Ian Fleming & Associates)**:** 51–70 (Professor I.M. Wired character).
Peter Visscher: 46.
Laurence Whiteley (at Folio)**:** 71, 72.

CREDITS

Edited by
Jackie Gaff
Designed by
Beth Aves
& Louise Jackson
Cover design
& artwork by
Jonathan Hair

Text pp. 1–70 & 87–92
© 1998 by Jacqueline Mitton
pp. 71–86 © 1998 by Michael Johnstone
Illustrations © 1998 by Walker Books Ltd.

All rights reserved.

First U.S. paperback edition 2000

Library of Congress Cataloging-in-Publication Data is available.

Library of Congress Catalog Card Number 98-7464

ISBN (hardcover)
0–7636–0492–5
ISBN (paperback)
0–7636–1042–9

10 9 8 7 6 5 4 3 2 1

Printed in Hong Kong

Every effort has been made to trace the ownership of all copyrighted material and to secure the necessary permission to reprint the material used herein. In the event of any question arising as to the use of any material, the publisher, while expressing regret for any inadvertent error, will be happy to make the necessary correction in future printings.

Candlewick Press
2067 Massachusetts Avenue
Cambridge, MA 02140